Living Colors
by Marcia S. Freeman

Rourke
Educational Media

rourkeeducationalmedia.com

All polar bears are white.

Most buffalo are brown.

Many frogs are green.

Some geese are gray.

A few birds are blue.

Very few snakes are yellow.

No pigs are purple.